INTRODUCTION FROM STEVE BACKSHALL

I'LL ALWAYS REMEMBER my first encounter with a shark. I was about eleven, on holiday and out snorkelling, when I saw a familiar silhouette. Not surprisingly my heart leapt, but then plunged as I realised the shark wasn't swimming off, but was circling around me. Panicked, I scrambled out of the water onto a rock, and sat there for three hours until I had horrific sunburn, and was forced to swim for shore. Now I know it was just a blacktip reef shark; was probably only a metre long, and less dangerous to me than a moody halibut! However, this set the store for a lifetime fascination – bordering on obsession – with these ancient ocean wanderers.

In the years since, I've dived with tiger sharks, blues, hammerheads, bronzies, silkies, makos, lemons, threshers, bulls, oceanic whitetips and even great whites without a cage, and never felt in any danger. I feel more threatened wandering round a big city at night!

Facts show, sharks are really not that dangerous to us: there are more people killed taking selfies than by sharks! However, our fishy friends are in big trouble, with as many as a quarter of a billion being taken from our seas each year. Sharks need pals; people that love them as much as me . . . and Jillian and Duncan who wrote this book.

So read these pages, learn about the legacy of the lords of the deep, discover that sharks can be weird and wonderful and possess amazing super powers. Perhaps dream yourself of a blue sea encounter with a shark or two. And then spread the word; let your friends and family know, that sharks are jaw-some, and that without our help they might disappear from our oceans.

Blue skies and calm seas, SB

ACC. No: 07078905

TIGER SHARK

(GALEOCERDO CUVIER)

TIGER SHARKS are often called 'rubbish bins' of the sea because they are not picky eaters. They've been found with random man-made items in their stomachs, including number plates and even a suit of armour. Parts such as bones, turtle shells and feathers are not easily digestible, so they throw up their own stomach to clean it out, leaving room for the next tasty treat.

© JILLIAN MORRIS

SUPER POWER:
STOMACH
OF
STEEL

They are named after their stripe-like markings, similar to a tiger's, which fade as they get older.

FAST FACTS

Can reach a **LENGTH** of 5.5 metres (18 feet).

They are **LONG DISTANCE SWIMMERS**. Research shows that adult males can make yearly round-trip journeys of **OVER 4,660 MILES** (7,500 kilometres) in the Northwest Atlantic.

Their **DIVERSE DIET** includes fish, sea turtles, sea snakes and even birds.

They give birth to **LIVE YOUNG** and can have 10–82 pups in a litter.

TIGER SHARK TOOTH

GREAT HAMMERHEAD SHARK

(SPHYRNA MOKARRAN)

The GREAT HAMMERHEAD SHARK'S odd shapped head and the location of their eyes actually helps them have super-powered vision. Not only can they see from side to side but also above, below, in front and behind.

Named for their hammer shaped head, which is known as the cephalofoil. They use it to pin down their prey.

SUPER POWER:

360 DEGREE VISION

© JILLIAN MORRIS

FAST FACTS

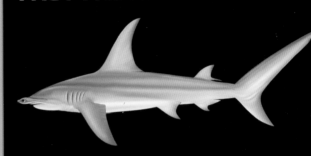

They are the **LARGEST SPECIES** of hammerhead shark and can reach a length of 6.1 metres (20 feet).

Despite having **VENOMOUS SPINES**, stingrays are still a favourite item on the menu for great hammerheads.

Their heads are covered with **ELECTRORECEPTORS** called ampullae of Lorenzini. These are often referred to as the shark's sixth sense. It is like having a **BUILT-IN METAL DETECTOR**, but instead of lost jewellery, they are finding food buried in the sand.

They can also **SWIM SIDEWAYS**. By turning on their side and swimming at an angle they become more efficient, using less energy to swim.

**GREAT HAMMERHEAD
SHARK TOOTH**

GREAT WHITE SHARK

(CARCHARODON CARCHARIAS)

GREAT WHITE SHARKS are another super athlete, migrating thousands of miles and able to perform some amazing aerial acrobatics. Like their relative the shortfin mako shark, they have the ability to keep their body warmer than the water around them, so their muscles are charged up and ready for bursts of speed, enabling them to rocket out of the water.

They feed on fish when they are young, adding seals and sea lions to their diet as adults.

SUPER POWER:
AERIAL ACROBATICS

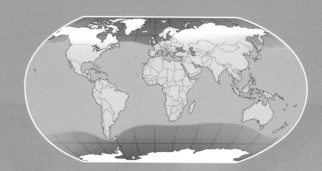

FAST FACTS

Can reach a **LENGTH** of 6 metres (19 feet) and weigh up to 2,268 kilogrammes.

They have their own **SOCIAL GROUPS** and interactions.

These ocean wanderers **MIGRATE** thousands of miles, with many returning to the same locations at the same time each year.

They can live at least **70 YEARS**.

GREAT WHITE SHARK TOOTH

NURSE SHARK

(GINGLYMOSTOMA CIRRATUM)

NURSE SHARKS have incredible suction power with some of the fastest jaws in the shark world. This suction has been said to be equal to that of ten vacuum cleaners.

They are bottom feeders, eating small fish, conch, lobster, snails, crabs, shrimp and squid.

© JILLIAN MORRIS

© JILLIAN MORRIS

THEY CAN **EVEN** **SUCK** A **CONCH** (A LARGE SNAIL) OUT OF ITS **SHELL.**

SUPER POWER:
SUPER SUCTION

They are a partially migratory species, meaning some migrate and others do not.

FAST FACTS

They can reach a **LENGTH** of 3.35 metres (11 feet).

These sharks can **REST** on the bottom of the ocean because they do not have to swim to breathe. They use their buccal (mouth) muscles to suck water in and **PUMP** it across their gills.

They have **NASAL BARBELS** which they use to find food on the bottom of the ocean floor.

Nurse shark pups are covered in **SPOTS**.

NURSE SHARK TOOTH

BULL SHARK

(CARCHARHINUS LEUCAS)

Most sharks live in saltwater, but BULL SHARKS can survive in brackish and fresh water as well. They are able to osmoregulate, which allows their body to adapt to less salt in the water. Bull sharks have been found over 621 miles (1000 kilometres) up a fresh water river.

© JILLIAN MORRIS

SUPER POWER:

FRESHWATER ADAPTABILITY

To survive in fresh water they pee more, which controls the salt levels in their bodies.

FAST FACTS

Can reach a **LENGTH** of 3.4 metres (11 feet).

They have the **STRONGEST BITE FORCE** of any shark that has been measured (stronger than a great white shark).

They have been seen in the same areas as **CROCODILES** and **ALLIGATORS** – and sometimes end up on their menu!

They give birth to **LIVE YOUNG**, which are usually born in estuaries or rivers.

BULL SHARK TOOTH

© JILLIAN MORRIS

GREENLAND SHARK

(SOMNIOSUS MICROCEPHALUS)

The slow-moving GREENLAND SHARKS are definitely not Olympic swimmers, but they will outlive all the other competitors. Scientists studied their eyes and used radiocarbon dating to determine they can live at least 272 years, with one shark being almost 400 years old. They become adults at 150 years of age!

SUPER POWER:

LONG
LIFE

© ALAMY

FAST FACTS

Can reach a **LENGTH** of at least 6.4 metres (20 feet).

Most become **PARTIALLY BLIND** from copepods, a parasite, attaching to their eye and causing damage.

They are definitely **NOT PICKY EATERS**, feeding on fish and marine mammals, but also scavenging on land animals such as dead reindeer or polar bears.

Known as a 'sleeper shark' because of their **SLOW SWIMMING**, these sharks move at an average pace of 0.76 miles-per-hour (0.3 metres-per-second).

GREENLAND SHARK TOOTH

They are a cold-water species found in the North Atlantic and Arctic oceans.

SWELL SHARK

(CEPHALOSCYLLIUM VENTRIOSUM) ////

SWELL SHARKS are able to glow thanks to a special protein in their skin. This protein glows neon green when activated by blue light. The human eye cannot see this, but other swell sharks can. Scientists use special cameras to capture images of their fascinating glowing ability.

THIS **GLOW** IS LIKE A **SECRET HANDSHAKE,** ONLY SEEN BY OTHER SHARKS WITH A SIMILAR **TYPE OF VISION!**

SUPER POWER:

GLOWS IN THE DARK

Named for its ability to swallow water and swell up in size.

FAST FACTS

Can reach a **LENGTH** of 88-109 centimetres (35-43 inches).

Can be found at **DEPTHS** of up to 457 metres (1500 feet) but is most often found in the range of 5-37 metres (16-121 feet).

When it **FEELS THREATENED**, this shark curls up and grabs its tail fin with its mouth - just like a **SHARK DOUGHNUT**. It can also gulp water into its stomach causing the shark to swell nearly double in size. If caught and brought above the surface of the water, it can do the same thing with air.

Females **LAY EGG CASES** and the pups (baby sharks) are about 15 centimetres (6 inches) when they hatch out.

SWELL SHARK TOOTH

COOKIE CUTTER SHARK

(ISISTIUS BRASILIENSIS)

Although they are small, COOKIECUTTER SHARKS dine on animals much larger than themselves, including whales, large fish, sea lions and even other sharks. They suction onto their prey and take a cookie sized bite.

© DEAN GRUBBS

SUPER POWER:
COOKIECUTTER JAWS

They have the largest teeth compared to body size of any shark.

FAST FACTS

Can reach a **LENGTH** of 50 centimetres (1.6 feet).

They are a **DEEP SEA** species found at depths of 1000 metres (3280 feet) during the day before moving to shallower depths at night.

They **SWALLOW ALL 25–31 TEETH** on their lower jaw in one go and grow new ones to replace them.

They have tiny light producing organs on their belly, which produce a greenish coloured **GLOW**.

COOKIE CUTTER SHARK TOOTH

SAND TIGER SHARK

(CARCHARIAS TAURUS)

SAND TIGERS are the scuba divers of the shark world. They are able to achieve neutral buoyancy by gulping air and holding it in their stomach. This prevents them from sinking when they stop swimming, instead they hover mid-water. When they are ready to move, they just fart to release the air.

They hang out with "friends" and are known to gather in groups of 20-80 sharks.

SUPER POWER:

MEGA FARTS

FAST FACTS

Can reach a **LENGTH** of 3.2 metres (10.5 feet).

These sharks are easily identified by their **TOOTHY SMILE**, with teeth pointing outwards even when their mouth is closed.

Babies **EAT** their smaller and weaker brothers and sisters while in the womb, leaving only two pups born per litter.

They have been seen hunting in groups, **WORKING TOGETHER** to herd schools of fish.

SAND TIGER TOOTH

PRICKLY DOGFISH

(OXYNOTUS BRUNIENSIS)

Shark skin is covered in very tiny v-shaped scales called dermal denticles.
These 'skin teeth' reduce drag, making it easier for sharks to swim.
The PRICKLY DOGFISH has very large dermal denticles,
which are visible to the human eye.
They make the shark appear
similar to an underwater
hedgehog.

Both of their dorsal fins have spines, adding weapons to their prickly suit of armour.

SUPER POWER:
ARMOUR PLATED

FAST FACTS

Can reach a **LENGTH** of 76 centimetres (30 inches).

Named for their **VERY LARGE** dermal denticles, which make them appear **PRICKLY**.

They are a **DEEP SEA SPECIES**, most commonly found at depths of 350–650 metres (1148–2132 feet).

They are **PICKY EATERS**, **ONLY** dining on the egg capsules of 'ghost sharks' (Chimaera).

PRICKLY DOGFISH TOOTH

© BRIT FINUCCI

GOBLIN SHARK

(MITSUKURINA OWSTONI)

GOBLIN SHARKS can catapult their jaws forward with a slingshot motion in order to grab prey. Stretchy ligaments allow their jaws to move forward and then retract. If your mouth could do this, you would be able to bite a piece of food hanging 18 centimetres (7 inches) in front of your face!

**SUPER POWER:
SLINGSHOT
JAWS**

They are named for their goblin-like appearance.

FAST FACTS

Can reach a **LENGTH** of 5.5 metres (18 feet).

They are a **DEEP SEA SPECIES** found at average depths of 270–960 metres (885–3149 feet).

Their skin is **TRANSLUCENT**, appearing pinkish-white because of tissue and blood vessels visable underneath.

Their **SLINGSHOT JAWS** can move forward at a speed of 3.1 miles-per-hour (5 kilometres-per-hour).

GOBLIN SHARK TOOTH

SMALLTOOTH SAWFISH

(PRISTIS PECTINATA)

SAWFISH have a saw on their face. They have a long snout (called a rostrum) lined with teeth. They use this to detect and then slash at schools of fish. Wielding their saw like a sword, they stun or injure their prey, making it easier to grab their lunch.

Sawfish are actually a ray, with their gills and mouth located on the underside of their body.

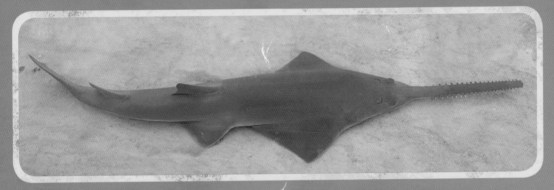

© JILLIAN MORRIS

SUPER POWER:

WEAPONISED FACE

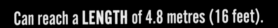

FAST FACTS

Can reach a **LENGTH** of 4.8 metres (16 feet).

Sawfish are some of the most **ENDANGERED** marine fishes in the world.

They have 7–14 **PUPS** per litter, with each pup being about 60–70 centimetres (2–2.2 feet) long at birth.

Pups are born with a **GELATINOUS SHEATH** over their saws to protect their mother.

SMALLTOOTH SAWFISH TOOTH

SHORTFIN MAKO SHARK

(ISURUS OXYRINCHUS)

SHORTFIN MAKO SHARKS are believed to be the fastest species of shark, swimming at estimated bursts of 45–60 miles-per-hour (72–96 kilometres-per-hour). Along with a torpedo shaped body, they have a specialised blood vessel structure that keeps their muscles warmed up and ready to chase their fast food (tuna and mackerel).

SUPER POWER:
BUILT FOR SPEED

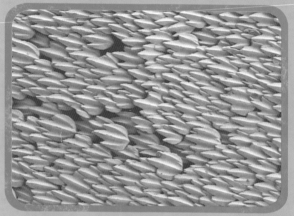

© GEORGE V LAUDER

LIKE **ALL SHARKS**, THEY ARE **COVERED** IN **DERMAL DENTICLES** WHICH ALLOW THEM TO **MOVE** THROUGH THE WATER MORE EFFICIENTLY. THIS **HELPS INCREASE** THEIR **SPEEDY SWIMS.**

They are aerial acrobats, using their warmed-up muscles to leap out of the water.

© RON WATKINS

FAST FACTS

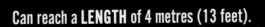

Can reach a **LENGTH** of 4 metres (13 feet).

They are **LONG-DISTANCE SWIMMERS**. One shark was tagged and swam over 13,000 miles (20,900 kilometres) in just under two years!

Despite their speed, they are one of the most **OVERFISHED** sharks in the world and their populations are declining, especially in the North Atlantic.

SHORTFIN MAKO SHARK TOOTH

PELAGIC THRESHER SHARK

(ALOPIAS PELAGICUS)

When a THRESHER SHARK swims quickly towards a school of fish and stops abruptly, its long scythe-like tail snaps forward at a speed of up to 30 miles-per-hour (48 kilometres-per-hour). This stuns its prey, making it easier to grab lunch!

SUPER POWER:
NINJA TAIL

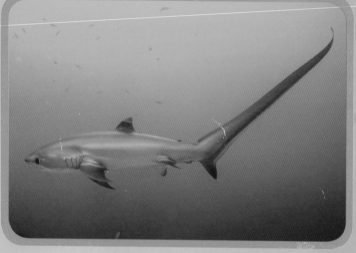

© ISTOCK

They prey on schooling fish, such as sardines and squid.

FAST FACTS

They are the smallest species of thresher shark, reaching a **LENGTH** of 3.65 metres (12 feet).

Their caudal (tail) fin can be as **LONG** as their body.

They have **TWO PUPS** per litter.

They are **BIG BABIES**, reaching up to 1.5 metres (5 feet) in length at birth. Whilst in the womb they eat other eggs, which is known as oophagy.

PELAGIC THREASHER SHARK TOOTH

INDEX

WANT TO LEARN MORE? – REFERENCE LIST.

Ebert, David & Fowler, Sarah & Compagno, Leonard. *Sharks of the World: A Fully Illustrated Guide.* Wild Nature Press, 2013.

Finucci, B., Bustamante, C., Jones, E.G. and Dunn, M.R. 2016. Reproductive biology and feeding habits of the prickly dogfish *Oxynotus bruniensis. Journal of Fish Biology* 89(5): 2326-2344.

Gruber, D., Loew, E., Deheyn, D. et al. 2016. Biofluorescence in Catsharks (Scyliorhinidae): Fundamental Description and Relevance for Elasmobranch Visual Ecology. *Sci Rep 6,* 24751. doi:10.1038/srep24751.

Hamady, L.L., Natanson, L. J., Skomal, G. B. and Thorrold, S. R. (2014) Vertebral Bomb Radiocarbon Suggests Extreme Longevity in White Sharks. PLoS ONE 9(1): e84006. https://doi.org/10.1371/journal.pone.0084006.

Lea, J. S. E. et al. 2015. Repeated, long-distance migrations by a philopatric predator targeting highly contrasting ecosystems. *Sci. Rep. 5,*11202; doi: 10.1038/srep11202.

Habegger, M. L., Motta, P. J., Huber, D.R. and Dean, M.N. 2012 Feeding biomechanics and theoretical calculations of bite force in bull sharks (Carcharhinus leucas) during ontogeny. *Zoology* 115(6): 354-364.

McComb, D.M., Tricas, T.C., & Kajiura, S.M. 2009. Enhanced visual fields in hammerhead sharks. *Journal of Experimental Biology* 2009 212: 4010-4018.

Meyer, C.G., O'Malley J.M., Papastamatiou Y.P., Dale, J.J., Hutchinson, M.R., Anderson, J.M, et al. 2014. Growth and Maximum Size of Tiger Sharks (*Galeocerdo cuvier*) in Hawaii. PLoS ONE 9(1): e84799.

Nakaya, K., Tomita, T., Suda, K., Sato, K., Ogimoto, K., Chappell, A., Sato, T., Takano, K. and Yuki, Y. 2016. Slingshot feeding of the goblin shark *Mitsukurina owstoni* (Pisces: Lamniformes: Mitsukurinidae) *Scientific Reports*, 6 DOI: 10.1038/srep27786.

Nielsen, J., Hedeholm, R., Bushnell, P., Brill, R., Olsen, J., Heinemeier, J., Christiansen, J., Simon, M., Steffensen, V., and Steffensen, J. 2016. Eye lens radiocarbon reveals centuries of longevity in the Greenland shark (*Somniosus microcephalus*). *Science.* 353. 702. 10.1126/science.aaf1703.

Oliver, Turner, Gann, Silvosa and Jackson. 2013. Thresher Sharks Use Tail-Slaps as a Hunting Strategy. PLoS ONE. https://doi.org/10.1371/journal.pone.0067380.

Rabaiotti, Dani And Nick Caruso. *Does It Fart?: the Definitive Field Guide to Animal Flatulence.* QUERCUS Publishing, 2018.

Vaudo, J.J., Byrne, M.E., Wetherbee, B.M., Harvey, G.M. and Shivji, M.S. 2017. Long-term satellite tracking reveals region-specific movements of a large pelagic predator, the shortfin mako shark, in the western North Atlantic Ocean. *Journal of Applied Ecology.* doi: 10.1111/1365-2664.12852

Watanabe, Y. Y., Lydersen, C., Fisk, A. T., and Kovacs, K. M. 2012. The slowest fish: Swim speed and tail-beat frequency of Greenland sharks. *Journal of Experimental Marine Biology and Ecology* 426–427: 5z11. doi: 10.1016/j.jembe.2012.04.021.

The goal of **Sharks4Kids** is to create the next generation of shark advocates through education, outreach and adventure. Their team of scientists, educators, conservationists and professional videographers create a unique opportunity for the next generation to learn why sharks need kids and kids need sharks. They provide a dynamic range of interactive educational materials and experiences for students and teachers. The website provides free lesson plans, activities, curriculum, videos and more. Field trips and science education days gives students a hands-on learning opportunity. Their outreach programmes connect scientists and conservationists directly to students either in person or virtually. From their launch in November 2013, the team has spoken to over 125,000 students in 47 countries. They believe students have a voice and can make a difference, so we must empower and inspire them to do so.

© STEPHEN BRAKE

JILLIAN MORRIS

is a marine biologist, shark conservationist, photographer, author and the founder of Sharks4Kids. She has travelled the world working on shark research, diving and media projects. She is a PADI Ambassadiver, named as an ocean hero by *Scuba Diving Magazine* and listed as one of the 18 most influential women in ocean conservation by *Ocean Geographic* magazine. Jillian loves sharing her passion for the ocean with others through education and media. She has run shark education and conservation programmes in nine different countries, teaching thousands of students about sharks, shark science and conservation. Her favourite shark is the great hammerhead. She lives in Bimini, The Bahamas with her husband and adopted pit bull.

DUNCAN BRAKE

is a marine biologist and award winning underwater cinematographer who has travelled, photographed and filmed extensively throughout the world. He has filmed for BBC programmes including *Shark*, *Blue Planet Live*, *Deadly 60* and *Naomi's Nightmares of Nature*. In addition to filming, Duncan indulges his passion for the oceans as the media director of education, outreach and adventure non profit, Sharks4kids as well as assisting on the board of the world renowned research station Bimini Sharklab. Duncan strives to use cameras and storytelling as valuable tools in capturing the natural world and share its mysteries with future generations to come. His favourite shark is the great hammerhead. He lives in Bimini, The Bahamas where he loves to film the incredible wildlife in his own backyard.

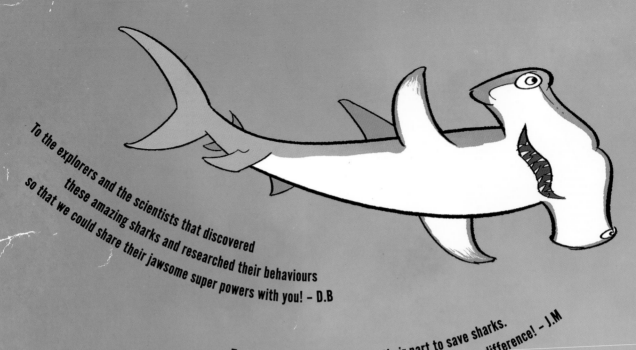

To the explorers and the scientists that discovered these amazing sharks and researched their behaviours so that we could share their jawsome super powers with you! – D.B

To all the kids out there doing their part to save sharks.
You have a voice and can make a difference! – J.M

SHARK SUPER POWERS is a uclanpublishing book

First published in Great Britain in 2020 by uclanpublishing in association with Sharks4kids
University of Central Lancashire, Preston, PR1 2HE, UK

Designed by Laura Neate

978-1-912979-16-5

1 3 5 7 9 10 8 6 4 2

A CIP catalogue record for this book is available from the British Library

Printed and bound in Great Britain by Page Bros Ltd, Mile Cross Ln, Norwich NR6 6SA